the story of
the design museum

the story of
the design museum

Tom Wilson

Asked to pick the single most rewarding achievement in my long design career so far, I would not hesitate to say founding the Design Museum in London. With one eye firmly on the future, however, moving the Design Museum to Kensington in 2016 has been overwhelmingly the most important and exciting. This is our time and this is our big moment. It has allowed all our dreams and ambitions for the museum to come true, creating a world-class space with the size and scope for the serious promotion and celebration of design and architecture in this country.

Creating the Design Museum was a hugely significant development for design in the UK and also for me personally—I suppose you could say it was my 'patriotic urge'. I'd been involved in selling design to the public and to industry for nearly thirty years but I had a fierce conviction that we could do more. It was the feeling that we could use intelligent design to change and improve Britain, so acting as a catalyst for social and economic change.

So in the early 1980s, with Habitat becoming a public company, I found myself with rather a lot of money for the first time and wanted to make a positive contribution to society. I tried to formulate ideas, and I kept coming back to the realization that design education was not being well understood by government and that it could be vitally important to the future of our country.

Paul Reilly was something of a mentor to me at that time and hugely influential in shaping my big idea. He headed up the Design Council, which was a truly vibrant place under his leadership, and over the years he did a tremendous job as the chairman of The Conran Foundation as we launched the Design Museum.

The Triennale exhibitions in Milan had always been stimulating for me, seeing at first hand the best of contemporary Italian and international design at a time when that country's designers were conquering the world. These were absolutely first-rate, influential design exhibitions that opened the eyes of both students and manufacturers to the best contemporary designed products in the world.

Paul and I agreed that a museum of industrial design of our own in Britain, featuring products from across the world, could be a very successful and influential project. I began to dream about creating a modest version of what I had been so inspired by in Milan, and set up The Conran Foundation determined to create a permanent home for the display of modern design.

Paul introduced me to Stephen Bayley, who was bursting with energy, ideas and ambition, and who would go on to become the first director of the museum. We approached Roy Strong, the director of the Victoria and Albert Museum, to see if he had any space, and he offered us a dark, dingy room in the basement that had formerly been used as the boiler room. There weren't even any stairs down to it, but I had always been seduced by quirky spaces and Roy said if we were prepared to convert the space ourselves then it was ours.

We created a simple white box that would become our home for the next five years, putting on something like twenty-five exhibitions with a vibrant and questioning approach. We became very popular very quickly, and we certainly learnt a lot about how to create a really serious museum. But after five years Roy and his curators needed the space back and we had to find a new home.

Around this time the big project in my life was the development of Butler's Wharf, and we thought: why shouldn't we take our museum and our ideas there with us? The London Dockland Development Corporation was keen to bring more cultural uses to the area, so we knew we would have its backing.

We identified an old derelict banana warehouse on the riverfront, which would become our home for the next twenty-five years. A team of Conran architects, headed up by Richard Doone, came up with a scheme that stripped back the brickwork and used the steel structure to create a simple, suitably Bauhausian building, which I thought was a perfect look for our new museum.

We opened in 1989, and since then the museum has always led the way in showing the work and inspirations of the most important designers and architects in the world—but more importantly we have supported and promoted the brightest young design talent. Our education and learning programme has connected with schools across the country, and we have the opportunity now to become the most important museum of design in the world. I founded the Design Museum to emphasize the importance of design in education, and more than quarter of a century later it fills me with great pride to see the galleries bursting with enthusiastic schoolchildren turning their own ideas into useful objects.

But now we have relocated to our wonderful new home in the magnificent former Commonwealth Institute building in Kensington. Designed originally by Sir Robert Matthew, it is an impressive listed building and the structure of the roof is extraordinary, an amazing geometric construction. The cathedral-like scale of what we have created at first made me gasp. I cannot praise the design team enough, who, led by John Pawson, have paid homage to the space as a wonderful piece of sculpture and created a building fit for the world's greatest museum of design.

It is a fine space in which to begin this bold and exciting new chapter in the Design Museum, under the excellent directorship of Deyan Sudjic and his team. We have three times more space than we had before, allowing us to show a wider range of exhibitions, and finally we have a dedicated area in which to properly showcase our world-class collection. We have created a library and a lecture theatre, both of which have significantly helped to extend our learning programme and go to the very core of the big idea I first shared with Paul Reilly all those years ago. I am certain that the sheer scale of our new Design Museum and the amount of space that we are giving over to education will become a vital part of Britain's future in design.

I also hope it will be embraced by industry and manufacturing, and be a place where government brings international visitors because they are proud to show off design in Britain. I believe it can be a catalyst that shows that quality of life can be improved significantly through intelligent design.

This is a remarkable opportunity to continue shaping Britain, and the new Design Museum can become the definitive voice of contemporary design, reinforcing our place as one of the world's leading creative economies. We can put design at the very heart of British creativity. Please join me and the design world on this exciting journey. Support us, enjoy our new exhibitions and our new home, and become part of the new Design Museum.

The Design Museum was founded by Sir Terence Conran in the belief that design has a vital part to play in shaping and understanding the world. The idea that design in the modern sense is a subject worth exploring in a museum was given its first and most powerful expression in 1851, when Sir Henry Cole and Prince Albert staged the Great Exhibition. This brought together the products of the Industrial Revolution from Europe and its colonies, as well as the Americas, and attracted a massive audience. It was the future, even if some visitors were appalled at some of the things that they saw.

Cole understood the economic importance of design, and also believed in its cultural significance. He set up the world's first museum of design, which was eventually named the Victoria and Albert Museum. He believed that there was such a thing as 'good design'–that there was an absolute standard by which taste could be judged, just as there was an absolute moral standard by which to judge behaviour. He inspired a number of other countries to establish what were mostly described as museums of decorative art, rather than design. They still exist in Vienna, Paris, Budapest and other cities. New York has the Cooper Hewitt. In Munich, there is the Neue Sammlung.

The term 'decorative art' is revealing. There is still a residual cultural hierarchy that sees the useful as somehow less culturally deserving of attention as art, which is not burdened by utility. If design is described as decorative art, then it is at least art of a kind that is worthy of inclusion in an institutional collection. In other institutions, which began to collect design in the twentieth century, curators where quick to say that good design could not be measured by commercial success. At the Museum of Modern Art, New York, one curator claimed that 'A frequent misconception is that the principal purpose of good modern design is to facilitate trade and that big sales are proof of excellence in design. Not so. Sales are episodes in the careers of designed objects. Use is the first consideration.' This can be seen as a defensive position. It is an apologetic argument for the place of design in a cultural institution against the scepticism of those who see it as lacking the creative integrity of art.

This book traces the story of the Design Museum's origins as the Boilerhouse Project inside the Victoria and Albert Museum to its new home in Kensington (in what was once the Commonwealth Institute that itself replaced the Imperial Institute). The Boilerhouse staged a very successful campaign to remind the V&A of its origins, and to restate the wider significance of design. Sir John Pope-Hennessy, director of the V&A in the 1970s had been dismissive of contemporary design. He was a scholar who knew a great deal about Italian Renaissance sculpture, but had little interest in the products of twentieth-century industrial design. If such things were allowed into the V&A at all it was under the guise of the increasingly marginalized 'circulating collections', that took second place to what were regarded as the more elevated study of artefacts untainted by concerns of modern commerce. That picture is completely transformed now.

Stephen Bayley, the founding director of the Design Museum, staged a series of provocative exhibitions at the Boilerhouse on such questions as taste, national characteristics and branding. They played an important part in transforming not just how the V&A regarded the contemporary world, but also in revitalizing other museums of decorative art. Rather than accept that design somehow had a lesser cultural significance than art, Bayley argued that in the twentieth-century design had supplanted art. Design had the ability to engage with a much wider public that remained largely unmoved by developments in contemporary art. Bayley somewhat mischievously suggested that were Michelangelo still alive, rather than carving marble tomb sculptures for a Medici pope he would be in Detroit modelling clay to design cars.

In its first incarnation in a converted banana-ripening warehouse next to Tower Bridge at Shad Thames, and since 2016 in the former Commonwealth Institute in Kensington, the Design Museum has been a platform for many views of what design can be. The architectural language used by the museum in its different buildings has significance in itself. In Shad Thames, a 1950s brick-and-concrete building was transformed by Richard Doone of Conran and Partners into a handsome tribute to the white walls of the Bauhaus. In Kensington, John Pawson and his team have carried out an exemplary restoration of a mid-century-modern landmark to give it a new life. The Design Museum has a collection that it is able to put on show free of charge for the first time in Kensington. It is displayed not as a conventional chronology, but in order to offer an insight into the significance of design from the point of view of the user and the maker, as well as the designer. It tries to show what a design means, as well as how it is made.

Alongside this, the museum explores all kinds of design and architecture through its exhibitions programme, its learning activities, its awards and its design residencies. It is interested in fashion as well as technology, in socially vital projects and speculative research, in designers who ask questions with their work as well as those who try to answer them.

Design is an endlessly fascinating subject because of the way that it is continually refiguring itself. It has its roots in the Industrial Revolution, and the growth of a distinct activity of design once the connection between user and maker had been broken by the machine. New methods of production have had the impact of radically changing that relationship. And new technologies have made design now as much concerned with how we interact with touchscreens as with physical objects.

The Design Museum sees itself as trying to offer some perspective on this rapidly changing landscape. It looks forward, more than to the past. It sees contemporary design and architecture as part of a wider cultural landscape, rather than as the exclusive preserve of the specialist or the professional.

Our role is to explore what an object means to the people who use it and make it, as well as what it does and how it is made. In that sense, our new home is also a kind of exhibit. Its architecture and its original purpose as a showcase for the British Commonwealth form part of its history, and that story is told in this book as well as that of the Design Museum's own origins—first at the V&A, then at Shad Thames, and now here in its new home where it continues to set the agenda for contemporary design and architecture.

from south kensington to shad thames

1

1   A young Terence Conran, relaxing in a basket chair that
    he designed, c.1950

Few designers have had more impact on everyday life in Britain than Terence Conran [1]. In his early career as a designer, he demonstrated an extraordinary entrepreneurial drive alongside a keen visual sense. Conran abandoned his studies in textiles at the Central School of Art and Design to work on the Festival of Britain in 1951. The next year, he established Conran & Company, which made furniture in a modern style. Inspired by a trip to France, Conran opened his first restaurant later that year, the Soup Kitchen in Chandos Place. This was followed by the Orrery, a Parisian-style brasserie on the King's Road [2]. As Conran's restaurant business grew, so too did his design work. Conran & Company expanded to become the Conran Design Group in 1956, offering interiors, product design and graphics as well as furniture.

Conran's restaurants brought the generosity of French cooking to a Britain that was just beginning to recover from the austerity of the post-war years. As the memory of rationing began to fade, it occurred to Conran that there was a niche for a different kind of home store for a generation who did not necessarily share their parents' tastes. His first shop, Habitat, opened on London's Fulham Road in 1964. From the outset, Habitat set out to be more than just a furniture shop. It combined European and American modernism with rustic authenticity, juxtaposing leather lounge chairs and tubular-steel furniture alongside Japanese paper lanterns, French earthenware and – in the early days – Braun consumer electronics. Customers identified with the style of life that Habitat embodied. They looked for elegant but low-maintenance homes with cutlery that did not need polishing, tables that looked good without tablecloths, and cookware that went straight from the oven to the table. One of Habitat's bestselling items was the duvet, a continental import that ended the tedious routine of making the bed. Habitat changed the way the British middle class lived, just as the department stores of the nineteenth century had done. Through the store displays and a catalogue full of seductively photographed interiors, Conran created a vision of a way of life that other people wished to live. In the words of the first catalogue, Habitat offered 'instant good taste ... for switched-on people' [3–4].

2

3

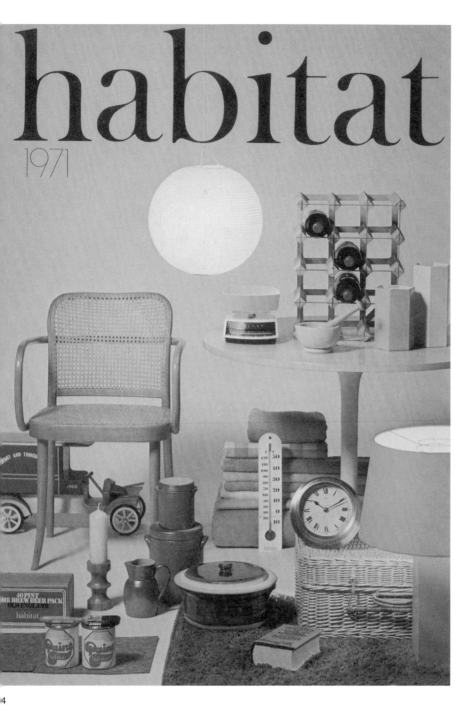

habitat

1971

2   The original Orrery Bar, 1954. The bar was named after   4   Habitat catalogue, 1971. Published like magazines,
     the astronomical instruments that fascinated Conran.   Conran's catalogues featured a wide range of
3   The opening of the first Habitat in Fulham Road, 1964.   beautifully-shot products and aspirational interiors.
     The staff wore uniforms designed by Mary Quant and
     had their hair styled by Vidal Sassoon.

5

Boilerhouse Project

6

5   Stephen Bayley during the early years of the
Boilerhouse Project, 1984
6   The Boilerhouse Project Logo, designed by
Flo Bayley, 1982

Habitat grew into an international chain, and its success propelled Conran into the public consciousness. Through his retail and restaurant businesses, Conran has done as much to introduce the concept of design to Britain as any designer or organization. However, his ambitions did not stop there. Education has always been close to Conran's heart; despite his own experiences as an undergraduate, he taught interior design at the Royal College of Art between 1957 and 1962, and held evening classes at the Central School of Art. Given that design was the key to improving the quality of everyday life, Conran believed that increased education in design was essential to support the creative infrastructure required. London had been one of the first cities in the world to pioneer design education, and if the British capital was to continue to be a centre for thriving industry and creativity then there needed to be a new institution that would create and sustain a discourse about contemporary industrial design.

The Conran Foundation

In 1978, Conran asked Sir Paul Reilly, director of the Design Council, to help him find ways to make design an essential part of public consciousness as well as government policy. Reilly introduced Conran to Stephen Bayley, an academic at the University of Kent whose exploration of contemporary design had been published by the Design Council [5]. Conran subsequently asked Bayley to undertake a feasibility study into the creation of a museum of industrial design, and funded a research trip around Europe and the United States. Bayley found that while New York's Museum of Modern Art and the Pompidou Centre in Paris had collections of industrial design, these tended to be subsumed within wider art collections. There was no major institution focused on industrial design. Conran decided to fill the gap.

The next step was to find a location. In 1980, Bayley approached Alan Bowness, director of the Tate Gallery at Millbank, about the possibility of a Conran-funded design wing along the lines of New York's Museum of Modern Art. According to Bayley, Bowness politely declined his offer on the basis that 'lampshades were not very exalting'. The derelict Battersea Power Station was also considered, as was a site at Willen Lake near

7   *Art and Industry: A Century of Design in the Products We Use*, exhibition poster, 1981. This was the first exhibition to be shown at the Boilerhouse.

Milton Keynes where Habitat was considering relocating its headquarters. In Bayley's imagination, industrial robots would 'rush up and down a warehouse lit by Holophane Prismatic Luminaires fetching Braun stereos off shelves for students to admire and analyze'.

In 1981, Conran floated Habitat on the stock market. The floatation gave him the resources to establish the Conran Foundation, a charitable trust committed to the promotion of design education. Shortly afterwards, Reilly introduced Conran and Bayley to Sir Roy Strong, the director of the Victoria and Albert Museum in South Kensington. Strong offered them the chance to test public interest in design in his museum. There were two possible locations: one, a dilapidated basement located at the centre of the museum; another in the former boiler-house site on the museum's western boundary, behind the distinctive Aston Webb screen on Exhibition Road. Conran and Bayley chose the latter site, and the Conran Foundation signed a five-year lease to establish the Boilerhouse Project, a space devoted to contemporary design [6].

The Boilerhouse Project

Shortly after signing the lease, Conran and Bayley set to work converting the disused boiler house into the most modern exhibition gallery in London. Designed by Conran Associates, the walls and floor of the Boilerhouse Project were lined with white tiles, and a gridded ceiling was installed with downlighters (also painted white) for maximum display flexibility. The effect was so clinical that Bayley later recalled that his office was scouted as a location for a television advert for aspirin.

The Boilerhouse Project was to be a testing ground for what a permanent design museum might be, and over the following years it staged a series of temporary exhibitions exploring the relationships between design, industry and commerce. Its ambition was to be 'light on its feet', so that it could respond to current events as they happened and take advantage of opportunities if they arose. The name was deliberately chosen to evoke associations with energy and the ferment of industry; as Bayley explained, the 'Boilerhouse Project' sounded 'like a play on Bauhaus, yet in a subtle, practical way it invokes technology'.

8

8   Elliot Noyes' petrol pump for Mobil Oil in the exhibition
Art and Industry, 1982

The Boilerhouse Project's approach was made clear by its inaugural exhibition, *Art and Industry: A Century of Design in the Products We Use*, which opened on 14 January 1982 [7]. Through a series of case studies, the exhibition celebrated the work of major designers and the corporations that brought them into being, including Raymond Loewy's duplicator for Gestetner, Ettore Sottsass's typewriters for Olivetti and Walter Dorwin Teague's work for Boeing. Featuring the first car to be shown in the V&A, *Art and Industry* was a clear signal that the Boilerhouse Project would be concerned mainly with 'designs from the real world'. The exhibition stood as a sharp contrast with the older museum's collections of medieval tapestries and Renaissance sculpture, despite the fact that the V&A had been established after the Great Exhibition of 1851 to promote the best of new design. One visitor even wrote of their shock at seeing Eliot Noyes' circular petrol pump for Mobil Oil displayed on a white pedestal [8].

Over the following years, the Boilerhouse Project housed a succession of popular and successful exhibitions. It featured shows on individual firms such as the Japanese electronics manufacturer Sony; personalities such as the British industrial designer Kenneth Grange; and design processes including the making of Ford's car, the Sierra. Other shows addressed more complex issues such as a history of taste, the use of robotics in everyday life and the ergonomics of hand tools. The Boilerhouse Project positioned itself at the forefront of new and contemporary design; it was the first gallery in London to show the work of the Italian avant-garde designers Memphis, and the first in Europe to showcase Japanese fashion designer Issey Miyake's intricately tailored clothes [9–12].

The project staged no fewer than twenty three exhibitions in the course of its five-year existence, and over its lifetime it was visited by more than 1.5 million visitors. However, its focus on popular culture sat uncomfortably with the V&A's curators, who were primarily committed to the decorative and applied arts. The last straw came in 1986, when an exhibition on the design and branding of Coca-Cola attracted more visitors than the rest of the museum. When Conran offered to turn the Boilerhouse

9

10

11

12

9   *The Past, Present and Future of Sony: An Exhibition of Japanese International Design*, exhibition poster, 1982

10 *Memphis: Milano in London*, exhibition poster, 1982. This was the first exhibition of Memphis designs in London.

11 *Issey Miyake: Bodyworks*, 1985. The Japanese fashion designer's first London show was described as 'theatrical, extravagant and glossy'.

12 *Hand Tools*, 1984. The wedge-shaped vitrines were designed by John Pawson. Visitors had to bend down to see the full range of objects on display.

THE CONRAN
FOUNDATION

13

13   The Conran Foundation promotional document adver-
      tising the establishment of the Design Museum
      at Shad Thames, 1987

Project into a permanent fixture, the V&A chose not to renew the lease.

Despite its short lifespan, the project played an important role in putting contemporary design on the agenda in Britain. As Bayley noted, it 'tapped into and demonstrated the existence of a latent interest in design'. Through its groundbreaking exhibitions and shows, the Boilerhouse Project paved the way for the establishment of the world's first museum devoted to the study of industrial design and contemporary architecture [13].

Butler's Wharf

In 1981, a consortium led by Conran won a bid for the mixed-use redevelopment of Butler's Wharf, an 11-acre site on the south bank of the River Thames. Lying just east of Tower Bridge, the plot comprised a dense group of Victorian warehouses, where ships once unloaded grain, sugar, tea and spices from across the world [14]. As container terminals forced shipping to move upriver during the twentieth century the warehouses fell into disuse, and after 1972 the area was mostly derelict. Conran's architectural practice, Conran Roche, converted a number of Victorian warehouses into apartments, while leading architects including CZWG and Michael and Patricia Hopkins were commissioned to design new commercial and residential complexes in the area.

In 1986, the Boilerhouse Project was renamed the Design Museum, and Butler's Wharf became its new home. The architect Max Gordon chose a former warehouse on Shad Thames with spectacular views of the Thames and Tower Bridge to house the new museum. The warehouse had most recently been a store for war-era Korean military supplies, but following a £7 million donation from the Conran Foundation it was remodelled by Conran Roche's Stuart Mosscrop and Richard Doone to become the new museum [15–16].

With its white walls and marble floors, glass-brick walls and generous balconies, the new Design Museum resembled a homage to the International Style of the 1930s. Standing in crisp contrast to the surrounding Victorian warehouses, the building's modern style was intended to be read as a statement of forward-looking purpose [17]. An early promotional brochure gave an idea of what visitors could expect from the new museum:

14

15

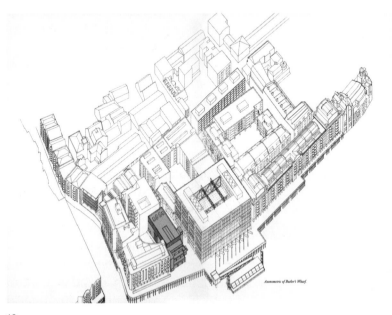

Axonometric of Butler's Wharf.

16

14 Victorian warehouses at Shad Thames, 1910
15 The Design Museum prior to its conversion, 1987.
    The warehouse was originally built to store and
    ripen bananas.
16 An axonometric drawing of Butler's Wharf, 1987. Conran
    bought a total of twenty-three derelict warehouses in the
    area. His vision for the renovation of the 11-acre site gave
    the Design Museum a prominent location by the Thames.
17 The Design Museum at Shad Thames just before its
    official opening, 1988

18

19

18   Terence Conran and Margaret Thatcher at the opening
      of the Design Museum, 1989
19   A wooden model of Le Corbusier's Voiture Minimum on
      the Design Museum's top-floor gallery, 1989

In a building of outstanding architectural character and quality on a remarkable site close to London's financial centre, the Design Museum will offer a range of resources which designers, industry and business may draw on to create better products, while providing students and the public with a stimulating environment in which to view, experience and evaluate design. When the Design Museum opens in Spring 1989 it will take the concept of the museum out of the nineteenth century and into the twenty-first century.

The Design Museum at Shad Thames

The Design Museum's Shad Thames site was opened by Prime Minister Margaret Thatcher on 6 July 1989 [18]. Bayley recalled eating miniature fish and chips in cornets made from the *Financial Times* and dancing with Akihiko Amanuma, one of the designers responsible for the Sony Walkman. In her opening speech, Thatcher challenged Conran and Bayley over their choice of the word 'museum', deliberately describing it as a 'Design Exhibition Centre' instead. Thatcher believed that the Design Museum's purpose was to be 'a living exhibition of design', arguing that 'a museum is something that is really rather dead'.

Despite Thatcher's concerns, Conran and Bayley continued to use 'museum' because it matched their ambitions for the study of industrial design to be taken seriously. The first floor was home to the Review, a changing display of new and innovative products. The first Review included a bus shelter, the latest Sony Walkman and Jasper Morrison's Ply Chair. The following year's Review featured a prototype mobile telephone by Jonathan Ive. A temporary exhibition space located on the same floor was named the Boilerhouse, in an evocation of the museum's first incarnation at the V&A. The top floor was devoted to the museum's collection of significant designs of the twentieth century [19]. A full-size wooden model of a car designed by Le Corbusier could be seen alongside Richard Sapper's kettle for Alessi, while an encyclopedic bank of Apple Macintosh computers contained Hypercard databases that visitors could use to explore designers, manufacturers and products. In keeping with the Conran Foundation's

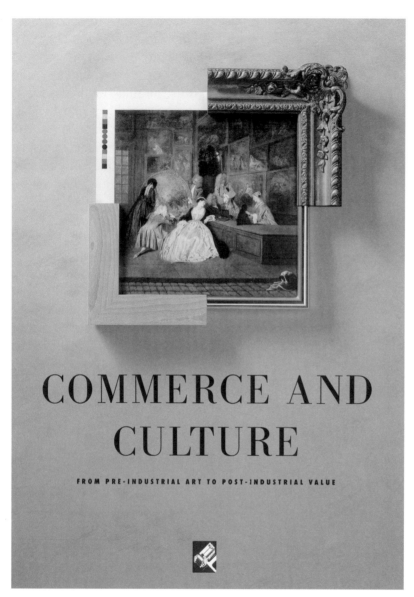

COMMERCE AND CULTURE

FROM PRE-INDUSTRIAL ART TO POST-INDUSTRIAL VALUE

20

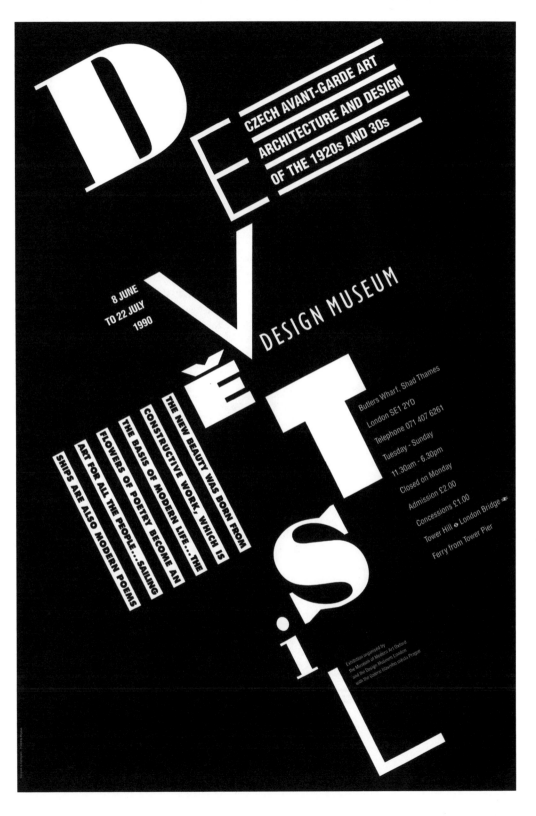

DEVĚTSIL

CZECH AVANT-GARDE ART
ARCHITECTURE AND DESIGN
OF THE 1920s AND 30s

8 JUNE
TO 22 JULY
1990

DESIGN MUSEUM

THE NEW BEAUTY WAS BORN FROM
CONSTRUCTIVE WORK, WHICH IS
THE BASIS OF MODERN LIFE...THE
FLOWERS OF POETRY BECOME AN
ART FOR ALL THE PEOPLE...SAILING
SHIPS ARE ALSO MODERN POEMS

Butlers Wharf, Shad Thames
London SE1 2YD
Telephone 071 407 6261
Tuesday - Sunday
11.30am - 6.30pm
Closed on Monday
Admission £2.00
Concessions £1.00
Tower Hill ⊖ London Bridge ⊖
Ferry from Tower Pier

Exhibition organised by
the Museum of Modern Art Oxford
and the Design Museum London
with the Galerie hlavního města Prague

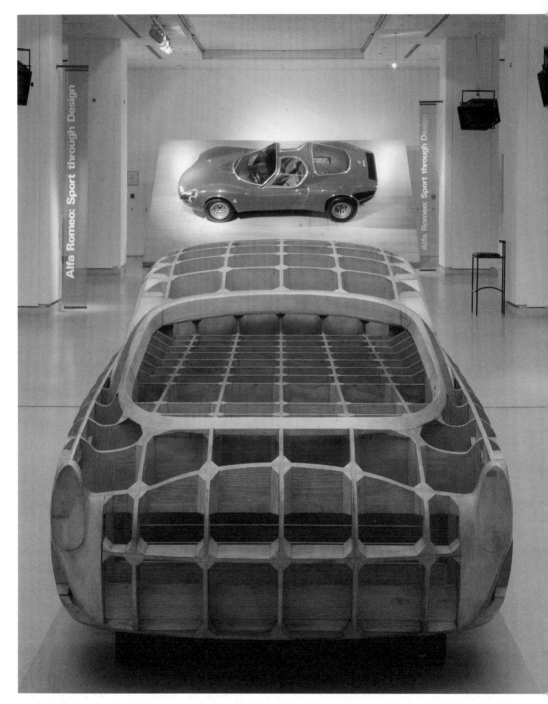

22

22   *Alfa Romeo: Sport Through Design*, 1991

mission, education was to be at the heart of the new Design Museum. A dedicated education programme was devised specifically to support 'increased understanding, evaluation and appreciation of design, thereby increasing accessibility of the museum for all visitors'. Lessons and workshops for students and families were held in the galleries, while a public programme consisting of films, conferences, talks and debates was aimed at adults.

The museum's first exhibition was *Commerce and Culture*, a challenging survey of the relationship between designers, manufacturers and shops through an examination of reproductions and originals, licensing, intellectual property and creativity [20]. 'Our modern muses are commerce, industry and technology, and we're trying to make a home for them,' wrote Bayley in the exhibition catalogue, 'Commerce and culture are all part of the same thing. The only difference between a museum and a department store is that in one of them, the goods are for sale.' By questioning traditional assumptions about design in contemporary culture, *Commerce and Culture* aimed to force a recognition that the boundaries between the commercial world, industrial production and cultural institutions were increasingly blurred. For Bayley, the new Design Museum's direction would be similar to that of a newspaper, surviving through commercial partnerships while still maintaining an independent, critical position.

Despite the optimism that accompanied its opening, the Design Museum's first few years at Shad Thames were a difficult time. Britain had entered a protracted depression, and the museum's early years were marked by funding difficulties. In spite of its troubles, Bayley's successor, Helen Rees, oversaw a wide-ranging programme of exhibitions that spanned the Devětsil avant-garde movement from Czechoslovakia, the design process of the Italian car manufacturer Alfa Romeo, and British graphic designers Abram Games and Hans Schleger [21–22]. Rees's last activity as director was to oversee a major exhibition on Eileen Gray, helping to bring the Irish furniture designer and pioneer of Modernist architecture back to public attention.

Designmuseum

23

24

25

26

23 The Design Museum's logo was re-designed by Mike
   Dempsey of CDT Design, 1995.
24 Curated by Catherine McDermott and designed by Nigel
   Coates, *The Power of Erotic Design* broke all previous
   visitor records, 1997.
25 *Ferdinand Porsche: Design Dynasty*, 1998
26 *Verner Panton: Light and Colour*, 1999

27

28

29

27   Thomas Heatherwick's eclectic collection for the annual
      Conran Foundation Collection exhibition, 2004
28   The cover for the Design Museum bulletin, featuring an
      image from the *Unseen Vogue* exhibition, 2002
29   *Alan Fletcher: Fifty Years of Graphic Work (and Play)*,
      2006. The London-based graphic designer passed
      away shortly before the opening of the exhibition.

In 1992, Rees was succeeded by Paul Thompson, the curator of the Review section [23]. One of Thompson's first acts was to introduce shows of contemporary practising designers to the museum, including a 1993 exhibition on Philippe Starck provocatively titled *Is Starck A Designer?* This was followed by major retrospectives on French architect and designer Charlotte Perriand, car designer Ferdinand Porsche and furniture and interior designer Verner Panton [24–26]. Another of Thompson's notable projects was an exhibition on the Bauhaus, the influential school of design at Dessau, which featured objects, prototypes and drawings that had only recently resurfaced in post-Cold War Germany. Thompson's tenure was also marked by the establishment of a Curating Contemporary Design MA in partnership with Kingston University, which continues today.

In 1993, the annual Conran Foundation Collection exhibition was established. Each year, an individual associated with design was invited to spend £30,000 on things that they would like to live with, reflecting their personal opinion of what they found innovative or inspiring. The first guest collector was product designer Ross Lovegrove, who purchased a range of items including a special edition Olympus camera, clothes hangers by Konstantin Grcic and a can of Gillette shaving gel. Subsequent guest collectors included industrial designers Jasper Morrison, David Constantine and Dutch collective Droog Design; journalist Tyler Brûlé; and television personality Carol Vorderman. The concluding exhibition was by Thomas Heatherwick, who assembled 1,000 everyday objects including corkscrews, lollipops and a bale of straw [27].

In 2001, Alice Rawsthorn became the museum's director. A former *Financial Times* journalist and Conran Foundation Collection participant, Rawsthorn bought an eclectic and vigorous programme to the museum. Retrospectives on well-known designers such as Manolo Blahnik, Alan Fletcher, Marc Newson and Peter Saville were accompanied by the first solo exhibitions of up-and-coming designers including the Bouroullec brothers, Fernando and Humberto Campana and Hella Jongerius [28–29]. In 2003, Rawsthorn introduced the Designer of the Year annual prize, which was won by Jonathan Ive,

30

31

32

33

34

35

36

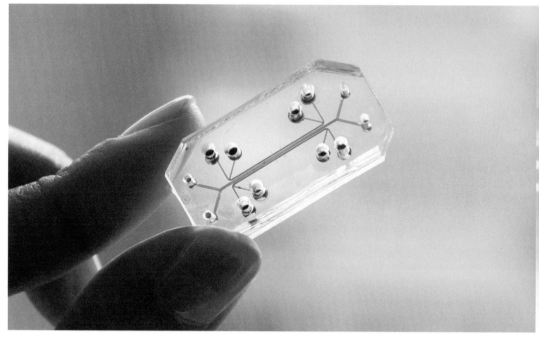

37

36   From 2008 onwards, beginning with the XO Laptop for the One Laptop Per Child project, the emphasis of the award has been on the design of the year, rather than the designer.

37   A Human Organs-on-Chip by Donald Ingber and Dan Dongeun Huh from Harvard University's Wyss Institute, 2015. The tiny microchip-like devices could revolutionize medical research by replacing animals in drug testing.

vice president of industrial design at Apple. This was a diverse competition, encouraging comparisons between disciplines ranging from jewellery to digital design. The success of the museum's exhibitions led to the establishment of an international touring-exhibition programme, as well as a number of educational initiatives ranging from children's creativity to adult learning.

As visitor numbers increased, the museum found itself at the centre of debates about the nature and definition of design. A 2004 exhibition on the floral arranger Constance Spry and the decision to award the 2005 Designer of the Year title to social entrepreneur Hilary Cottam sparked some very public discussions on the topic. Conceptions of design had changed since 1989, and the museum was increasingly moving beyond the idea of promoting mass-produced objects to engage with broader questions of what design might mean.

In 2007, Deyan Sudjic, a critic, editor and curator, became the Design Museum's fifth director. Sudjic introduced a Kunsthalle model in which the entire museum was devoted to a rolling programme of exhibitions, starting with retrospectives on Luigi Colani, Ettore Sottsass and the first British solo show on architect Zaha Hadid [30–31]. Since then, the Design Museum has approached the subject of design from a number of different perspectives. It combines historical surveys and thematic exhibitions with monographic profiles of key designers, including architects David Chipperfield and Louis Kahn; product designers Dieter Rams and Patricia Urquiola; and fashion designers Matthew Williamson, Hussein Chalayan and Paul Smith. An exhibition on Christian Louboutin was the museum's most popular show, breaking all previous visitor records [32–35].

The Designer of the Year award evolved to become the annual Designs of the Year competition in 2008, showcasing the most innovative, interesting and forward-looking designs from around the world. The first competition was won by the rugged yet affordable XO laptop, designed by Yves Béhar. Recent winners include a folding electrical plug, a redesigned lightbulb and the Human Organs-on-Chips, which mimics the complex function of living human organs [36–37].

38

39

38   Asif Khan, Designer in Residence, 2010. His work, *Harvest*, proposes the use of London's plant life as a raw material for everyday products.

39   Bethan Wood, Designer in Residence, 2010. Made from repurposed crates and packaging material, the *Particle* furniture range was inspired by Butler's Wharf's history as a centre for worldwide shipping and trade.

40

40   *Mariscal: Drawing Life*, 2009. After twenty-five years and over one hundred exhibitions, the Design Museum at Shad Thames finally closed its doors in June 2016.

With the continuing support of the Conran Foundation, the Design Museum's commitment to education
remains strong. The Designer in Residence programme
was established in 2007 to support emerging talent
[38–39]. In 2010, the museum launched the national
Design Ventura competition, which champions creative
thinking by challenging secondary-school students to
design a product. In 2011, the Design Museum received full
museum accreditation from the Arts Council, confirming
its importance in teaching the value of design.

Return to Kensington

In its twenty-five years at Shad Thames, the Design
Museum has staged over one hundred exhibitions,
welcomed over five million visitors and showcased some
of the world's most important designers [40]. However,
its increasing visitor numbers and learning activities
meant that it was rapidly outgrowing its home. It did not
have the facilities to cater for the needs of schools and
other groups, while the exhibition galleries were simply
not large enough to meet the museum's ambitions.

A number of options for an expanded site were considered, including King's Cross and Potter's Field next to
London's City Hall. A plot behind Tate Modern was a possibility, and a return to the V&A was briefly countenanced.
In 2008, the Design Museum received an offer to move
to the former Commonwealth Institute in Kensington.
The building had been acquired by property development firm Chelsfield, who planned a residential complex
on the site but needed a long-term occupant for the
Grade II* listed structure to secure planning consent.

In 2016, the Design Museum returned to Kensington.
It now occupies one of the most important post-war
buildings in London. John Pawson's refurbishment of the
spectacular exhibition hall has given the museum three
times as much space in which to show a wider range of
exhibitions. The museum now has the facilities to support
an extended learning programme including an auditorium, a library and specially equipped design studios.
The larger site also means that the museum's collection
can now be free to the public for the first time. From its
beginnings as the Boilerhouse Project, the new Design
Museum is uniquely placed to celebrate London as one
of the leading design centres in the world.

the story of the
commonwealth institute

1

1   The Imperial Institute nearing completion, 1892

Ever since the Great Exhibition of 1851, there had been proposals to build a permanent institution dedicated to the British Empire [1]. The idea was stoked by the fervour for exhibitions in the late nineteenth century. The Colonial and Indian Exhibition, for example, attracted over five million visitors in the six months that it was open in 1886. Following its success, the Prince of Wales announced plans for an 'Imperial Institute' that would carry on the work of the Exhibition as part of Queen Victoria's approaching Jubilee celebrations. A plot of land was identified in South Kensington, in the centre of the imperial axis running through the Natural History Museum, the Royal Albert Hall and the Albert Memorial [2].

Despite the prince's convictions, there were doubts about what the Institute's purpose would be. When an architectural commentator reviewed each of the six competition designs for the new Institute in 1887, he remarked on the variety of designs on show. 'As the world has not yet seen an "Imperial Institute" and no one appears yet to know precisely what it is for,' he wrote, 'it seems very much like asking six palaeontologists to furnish plans and elevations for a dodo, without supplying them with bones to evolve it from.' In June 1887, Thomas E. Collcutt's entry was selected as the winning design. Construction took six years, and the Institute was opened by Queen Victoria in May 1893 [3].

The Imperial Institute's purpose was to carry out research into the commercial use of raw materials. In many ways, it was also a celebration of Britain's imperial might. The exhibition galleries were, first and foremost, a stocktaking of natural resources from across the empire. In 1887 the poet Lewis Morris was asked to compose an 'Imperial Ode', which went:

> Here, in the stately chambers everywhere,
> And corridors with veined marbles, fine,
> The treasures of the wood, the sea, the mine,
> And kindly fruits our wide dominions bear,
> And corn, and oil, and wine …

Despite the fanfare that accompanied its opening, the Institute was not popular with either the British public or the empire it claimed to serve. The dominions and the

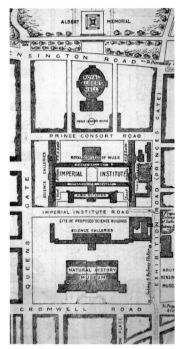

2

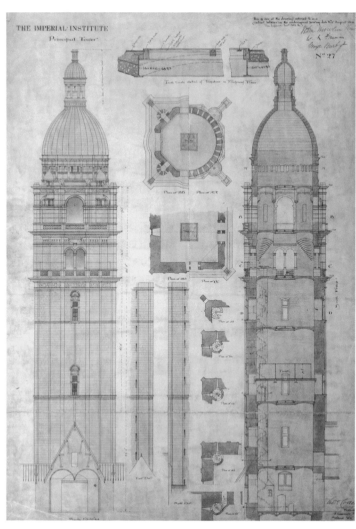

3

4

5

6

2   Imperial Institute site plan, 1887. Built on the former
    grounds of the Royal Horticultural Society, the Imperial
    Institute occupied a prominent location in South
    Kensington.
3   The Imperial Institute was designed by architect
    Thomas E. Collcutt in a neo-Renaissance style, 1887

4   The Ceylon gallery in the Imperial Institute, 1893
5   The Diorama Studio, 1893
6   Raphael Roussel's diorama of a Jamaican banana
    plantation, 1927

7

7   *At The Imperial Institute; Empire Under One Roof*,
poster designed by Herry Perry for London Transport
and the Underground Group, 1927

colonies were disappointed to see it located in South Kensington instead of the trading epicentre of the City of London, and many withheld their contributions after allegations of financial impropriety. In order to service its debts, the Institute introduced a number of popular entertainments aimed at paying audiences, including music evenings in the gardens and live demonstrations of motor cars in its quadrangles. These were, however, unsuccessful in attracting visitors.

Despite the fanfare that accompanied its opening, the Institute had to borrow heavily in order to complete its expensive building works. By 1899, its financial position had become desperate. The Prince of Wales approached Lord Haldane of his Privy Council to ensure its survival. Haldane arranged a deal whereby, in return for servicing its debts, the government would take over the Institute's lease. Half of the building was then sublet back to the Institute free of charge, while the University of London took over the other half of the premises. By 1901 the financial position was secure, but the Institute's work in developing the commercial and industrial resources of the Empire now overlapped with the Board of Trade. The governing body subsequently accepted that the Institute should be transferred wholly to the government, and an Act of Parliament was passed in 1902 to allow the Board of Trade to take over the Institute's management. For the next few years, responsibility for the Imperial Institute was transferred between several government departments, including the Colonial Office and the Department of Overseas Trade.

Following the patriotic fervour of the British Empire Exhibition at Wembley from 1924 to 1925, the Imperial Institute was given a new lease of life. Outdated displays of wool, minerals and grains were replaced by illuminated dioramas that magically appeared to replicate the empire in miniature. The exhibition galleries became a tour around the world, taking visitors to places they had never been and in all likelihood would never be able to go. Through dioramas of faraway landscapes and bronze statuettes of British explorers, soldiers and administrators, the essential components of an imperial narrative made itself felt throughout the exhibition galleries [4–6]. As curator Herbert Spooner put it:

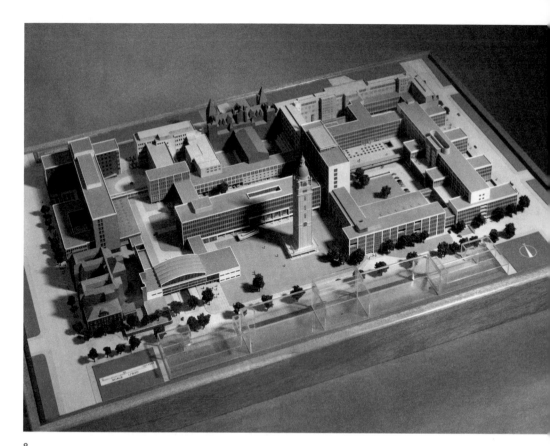

8

9

8   Norman and Dawbarn's architectural model for the
redevelopment of Imperial College, 1957. The Institute's
central tower was retained as a result of protests led by
Sir John Betjeman.

9   An aerial view of Holland Park, the new site of the
Commonwealth Institute, 1954

From being devoted primarily to the display of an index collection of the empire's commercial resources the Galleries have now become 'The Storyland of Empire'.

Such 'stories' explained Britain's rise as an imperial power as a logical consequence of an exceptional British character. The hope was that a visit to the exhibition galleries would invest visitors with a sense of national pride concomitant with imperialism [7].

From South Kensington to Holland Park

After World War II, demands for independence began to accelerate across the empire. India won its independence in 1947, and over the following decades Britain's empire was gradually dismantled. In the context of the emergence of a new Commonwealth, the *Evening Standard* reported that the Imperial Institute's reputation was that of an 'empire shrine' which 'does not keep pace with empire changes and seems to have its mind fixed too firmly on the past'.

In 1954, the British Government gave the land on which the Imperial Institute sat to the Imperial College of Science and Technology, which had been earmarked for rapid growth and development. Educating the next generation of nuclear scientists and aeronautical engineers was seen as more important for national prosperity than the empire, which was increasingly viewed as anachronistic and politically embarrassing in the modernizing ethos of the time. The architectural firm of Norman and Dawbarn was asked to plan Imperial College's redevelopment on the assumption that the Imperial Institute would be demolished. As the rector of Imperial College put it, the new college 'must accommodate the complex instruments and machines of modern science and technology', and, as such, would not be made of 'bricks and mortar' but of 'steel and concrete' [8].

In July 1956, a 3½-acre site became available in Holland Park, and the government moved quickly to secure it. It was further from central London than the Institute would have preferred, but they conceded that the leafy environs of Holland Park would allow them to occupy 'first-class surroundings' [9]. Legislation was passed later that year to enable the move from South

10

10 A representative from the Ceylon High Commission discusses a relief map of Ceylon with Kenneth Bradley, James Gardner and sculptor Kenneth Gilham, 1958.

Kensington, and was used as an opportunity to change its name to the Commonwealth Institute.

The Tent in the Park

The language of modernity was crucial for the new Commonwealth Institute. Although the board of governors had previously expressed a wish to remain at South Kensington, they now conceded that the conception of the Commonwealth as it stood today, '…and as we hope it will be in the future cannot be expressed in a building designed to glorify Victorian Imperialism'. By declaring that the new building should, first and foremost, 'be conceived in terms not of the past but of the future', they were placing their faith in the potential of modern architecture to act as a signifier of renewal and new beginnings.

Given the government's desire to accelerate Imperial College's expansion, an architectural competition for the new Commonwealth Institute was seen as an unnecessary impediment. In July 1957, Robert Matthew Johnson-Marshall & Partners (RMJM) were chosen on the strength of their post-war work at the London County Council, in particular the Royal Festival Hall on London's South Bank. Not only did the new building have to be constructed as quickly as possible, but it had to be cheap as well. The Institute had no capital funds of its own, and since its new home was to be paid for with public money the government wanted to prevent 'an extravagant or a luxurious building'. The cost limit was eventually set at £4 5s 0d. Although higher than originally proposed, this was still significantly lower than the £7 10s 0d to £9 10s 0d allocated for Imperial College and the £8 10s 0d budgeted for the new Royal College of Art.

Despite the stringent budget, the architectural brief allowed for considerable creative freedom, calling for a 'building of the most modern design, which is beautiful in itself, in harmony with its woodland setting, and functionally efficient'. The initial concept for the new Institute arose during discussions between Stirrat Johnson-Marshall, the RMJM partner in charge of the project, and Kenneth Bradley, the Institute's director [10]. From their dialogue, they resolved that the exhibition galleries should be architecturally dominant, with displays on an equal footing with one another, and laid out in a single space in the tradition of international exhibitions.

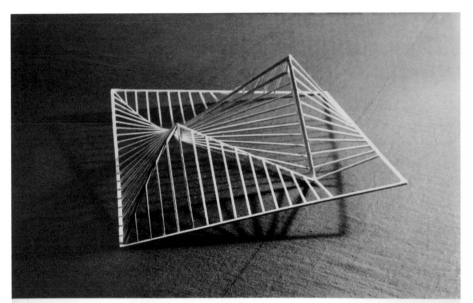

MODEL 6.   Oblique view 2.

510 / φ 7.

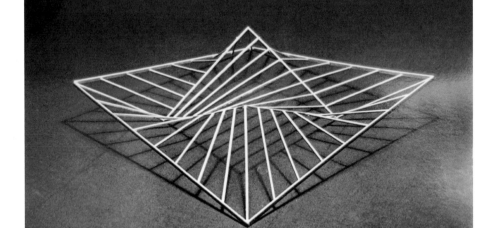

MODEL 4. High point axis — high level view.

510 / φ 12.

11–12 Various engineering test models were made for the Commonwealth Institute's roof, c.1957–8. After exploring several options, architect Roger Cunliffe and structural engineer Alan Harris settled upon a hyperbolic paraboloid shape.

13 The reinforced concrete spars in place, October 1961. The first spar took half a day to install but as builders got used to the process, the time taken was reduced to half an hour.

14

14   RMJM architectural model for the Commonwealth
        Institute, c.1958

These ideas led Johnson-Marshall to conceive of the new building as a large, uninterrupted space that would enable freedom of movement around the galleries.

Stirrat Johnson-Marshall's concepts were largely developed and translated into built form by others. The Institute project was led by Peter Newnham, who took charge from the drawing-board stage and saw it through to completion. The job architects were Roger Cunliffe, Tim Sturgis and Jack Gibb, while the engineering and structural work was carried out by Alan Harris and James Sutherland. The landscaping of the site was developed by Maurice Lee, an RMJM associate. At Lee's instigation, the distinguished landscape architect, Dame Sylvia Crowe, was invited to join the project team as work progressed, and to fine tune RMJM's original layout for the Institute's grounds. Among other things she proposed a sculpture garden that remained unrealized.

The task of providing a form for the new building fell to Cunliffe, who had experimented with cable-stayed roofs while a student at the Architectural Association. At the time, there was considerable interest within architectural circles in gravity-defying, shell-form concrete roofs. The Spanish-born engineer Félix Candela was particularly admired for his experiments with astonishingly thin concrete shells. In 1958, Bradley and the RMJM team travelled to the Brussels World's Fair, where they would have seen a number of exciting reinforced-concrete structures including the thin shells of Iannis Xenakis's Philips Pavilion, held in place by tensile-steel cables. They would also have been aware of Jørn Utzon's concrete hulls for the Sydney Opera House, which began construction in March 1959.

Working closely with Alan Harris, Cunliffe produced various shapes and models that ranged from 'engineers' shells' to freely curving 'sculptural shells' [11–12]. Of these, James Sutherland wrote that the engineers' shells were 'easy to design and to build, but looked dull, while the freer forms looked exciting but were almost impossible to calculate'. Eventually, they settled on a large hyperbolic-paraboloid shell supported by four smaller paraboloids. There were several advantages to this shape. Firstly, it was relatively economical to build. Despite its apparent complexity, a hyperbolic paraboloid

15

16

17

66

18

15   The Commonwealth Institute's roof under construction, July 1961

16   The central shell under construction, July 1961. It was made with light reinforced concrete and was only three inches thick in the middle.

17   Woodwool panels being placed on the roof, October 1961

18   Installing the reinforced concrete spars, 1961. These supported the central concrete shell.

19

19   A postcard showing the completed building, 1962

describes a ruled surface, with two straight lines running through any given point. This meant that concrete could be poured onto an angled grid of straight beams instead of expensive curved shuttering [13]. Secondly, a hyperbolic-paraboloid shell requires just two internal load-bearing columns, allowing for a clear, unbroken expanse inside. Thirdly, the shape's abstract geometry appeared free of negative connotations of imperialism and, as such, could be made to fit positive narratives of community and forward-looking optimism. The Institute's press department, for example, ebulliently described the roof as 'a double-peaked tent... soaring up and outwards to the sides to give an effect of lightness and movement'. The tent-in-the-park analogy was endlessly repeated by the press, while the *Manchester Guardian* evocatively described it as 'something like a square of ocean' [14].

Work began on site in October 1960. The complex shape of the roof could not be easily calculated through straightforward mathematical means, so a model was tested at the Cement and Concrete Association's research laboratory in Buckinghamshire. This was one of the earliest uses of electronic computer systems in testing reinforced-concrete structures. The test found that while concrete would be suitable for the central shell, it would not work for the side shells. As a result, James Sutherland had to redesign the roof while construction was proceeding. His solution was to use radiating spars made from precast, post-tensioned concrete beams overlaid with woodwool slabs. In this way, Cunliffe's original concept was adapted to become a single, central shell with four side 'warps' [15–18].

By October 1962, the building was finished [19]. The Commonwealth Institute headquarters was the most significant modern building to be completed in London since the Royal Festival Hall. In his autobiography, Bradley wrote that it 'would be the first building in the world to represent the unity in diversity that is the Commonwealth and to express its meaning. For such a purpose it must be beautiful and made of fine materials'. Given the Institute's stringent budget, the only way it could achieve Bradley's ambition was to appeal for gifts-in-kind from across the Commonwealth. A 1962 handbook was evocative in its list of materials used in the new building:

20

20 The Jehanghir Room was named after Cowasji
Jehanghir Readymoney, a Parsi philanthropist
from Bombay, 1962.
21 James Gardner's sketch for the East Pakistan
court, c.1960

22

23

22   The entrance to the Commonwealth Institute, 1962
23   An elevated view of the exhibition hall, 1962. The white
       marble on the central dais was salvaged and reused in
       the Design Museum's new home.

The hardwood floors of the exhibition galleries are made of opepe and sapele from Nigeria and Ghana respectively...The timbers used in the Western Entrance foyer are all Australian, the wood block floor of jarrah, the mullions of Tasmanian oak, and the panelling of figured black bean...The Board Room and adjoining Jehanghir Room on the first floor have floors of loliondo from Uganda and slatted ceilings of obeche from West Africa [20].

In addition, 25 tons of copper was given by the Northern Rhodesia Chamber of Mines as sheeting for the roof. The use of materials was intended to suggest that the building was a cooperative endeavour by the countries of the Commonwealth. Selecting building materials for symbolic reasons is a long standing architectural tradition.

The Next Best Thing

Stirrat Johnson-Marshall considered the Commonwealth Institute's exhibition galleries to be so integral to the building's character that he insisted on the appointment of exhibitions designer James Gardner at an early stage of the project [21]. With his extensive experience – including *Britain Can Make It* of 1946; the Festival of Britain in 1951; and, most recently, the British Pavilion at the 1958 Brussels World's Fair – Gardner was one of the country's most important post-war exhibition designers. Working closely with Bradley and Johnson-Marshall, his task was to develop the spatial arrangement and narrative treatment of the exhibition galleries. In many ways, this was almost as complicated a task as designing the building itself; there were to be forty-four courts in total, each of which had to have its own distinctive character. As Bradley remarked, 'visual harmony was going to be a problem'.

After passing through an introductory gallery, which emphasized Britain's role in the making of the Commonwealth, visitors turned a corner onto a bridge leading to a raised platform in the centre of the exhibition hall. The effect was to see the whole of the Commonwealth rising around them in three illuminated tiers [22–23]. Each country could be recognized from the central platform by a 'characteristic feature': banana trees decorated the Caribbean, a brightly coloured moon-kite soared above Malaya, while a Chinese dragon flew over Hong Kong. If

General layout. British Guiana
COMMONWEALTH INSTITUTE

24

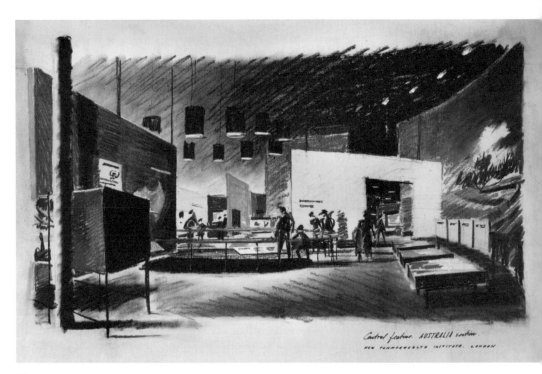

Central feature. AUSTRALIA section.
NEW COMMONWEALTH INSTITUTE. LONDON.

25

74

26

27

24 James Gardner's sketch for the British Guiana
    court, c.1961
25 James Gardner's sketch for the Australia court, c.1961

26 Barbara Jones painting a mural for the East Pakistan
    court, 1962
27 A stuffed Bengal tiger in the East Pakistan court, 1962.
    The tiger was shot especially for display.

28

28   A view of the first- and second-floor galleries, 1962

the presentation of empire depended on the encyclopedic assemblage of natural resources, then the projection of the Commonwealth depended on the assemblage of national identities within an equitable framework. While the intention was to create a layout that did not suggest any kind of hierarchy, and which allowed visitors to choose their own route through the displays, inevitably not all member states of the Commonwealth could be allocated equal amounts of space. The larger installations were on the lower levels [24–26].

Like the Imperial Institute before it, a visit to the Commonwealth Institute allowed the London public to see the world in a single afternoon. As the queen noted in her opening speech on 6 November 1962:

> …between us, my husband and I have seen more of the Commonwealth than almost any people alive …Unfortunately, it is not possible for the people of Britain to travel quite so extensively; but this building provides the next best thing.

Entering the exhibition galleries, visitors were immersed in the signs and symbols of the countries of the Commonwealth. Bougainvillea flowers adorned the Caribbean, orchids grew in the Singapore court and eucalyptus trees dotted Australia. Softly played music could be heard across the galleries, while the scent of cloves filled the Zanzibar court. Taxidermic specimens of birds and animals dotted the galleries, and children were encouraged to touch and stroke stuffed lions and tigers [27–28].

The opening of the Commonwealth Institute was positively received by the national press. For one journalist, 'the sheer bulk of things to be seen and places to be visited sweeps one off one's feet and back to childhood'. Despite the new organization's emphasis on modernity and forward-looking progress, many of the displays came from the Imperial Institute that preceded it. These included dioramas and statuettes that were by then more than thirty years old. This had the perhaps unintended effect of confirming received notions of the past as representative of the present, rather than challenging the public to think about the Commonwealth in new and different ways.

29

29   Archigram's visualization for Instant Malaysia, 1973.
The main attraction was a climate simulator, allowing
visitors to 'experience the heat of the jungle and the
cool breezes of the tea plantations'.

Changing Commonwealth

The Institute's relationship with the Commonwealth itself was vague and not clearly defined. In many ways, the Commonwealth's support of the Institute could be characterized as one of international diplomacy at a time of increased worldwide tension; if one country were to withdraw its support of the Institute, the risk was that this might be interpreted as a matter of political significance by other members. For its first decade at least, therefore, the Commonwealth Institute's exhibition galleries represented a carefully calculated show of unity.

However, the Institute could not maintain this impression for long. Constitutional changes were happening so quickly across the empire that it was difficult to keep up with the necessary alterations. Gardner continued to work as a consultant designer, but his efforts to maintain a consistent visual style were gradually undermined as countries became independent and sought to take control of their own displays. In 1973, Malaysia commissioned Archigram to present it as an industrially progressive nation. 'Instant Malaysia' featured a climate simulator that increased the ambient temperature and humidity before cooling down with fans, allowing visitors to experience the 'heat and humidity of the Malay jungle and the cool winds after the monsoon' [29].

As the Commonwealth began to assert itself as an organization concerned with international social justice, a gradually widening schism began to develop between it and the Commonwealth Institute's displays. As the *Guardian* noted in 1986, 'there was no hint of the real tensions among Britain and its former colonies in the exhibition galleries. On three highly polished floors … the harmony runs from Antigua to Zimbabwe'. Perhaps as a result of the difficulties inherent in representing the political idea of the Commonwealth in built form, the Institute began to focus instead on the promotion of multiculturalism through dance, music and art performances.

Decline and Renewal

In 1993, the centenary year of the opening of the Imperial Institute, the Foreign Office announced they would be cutting the Commonwealth Institute's grant-in-aid. The Foreign Office agreed to fund the Institute with a steadily reducing grant until 1999 in order to give them time

30

31

30–31   The derelict Commonwealth Institute before its
conversion into the Design Museum, 2012

to secure private funding. The institute subsequently redesigned the exhibition galleries as The Commonwealth Experience, featuring flight-simulator rides and interactive attractions designed to attract paying audiences. However, visitor numbers were disappointing and the galleries closed in 1998. From 2000, the building was used mainly as a trade and conference centre.

The Institute's financial difficulties were exacerbated by a building that was in desperate need of repair. The experimental nature of the roof, coupled with cost-cutting at the construction stage and a significant lack of upkeep had left the organization with a legacy of serious difficulties. When strong winds caught the upper slopes of the roof they created swirling currents, causing a drumming effect that proved too great for the fixings to hold. As a result, many of the copper sheets came loose from the substrate underneath, and had to be held down with scaffolding poles and weighted cables. Because of the roof's shape, rainwater collected at its lowest points where they drained through six-inch drainpipes embedded in the internal columns. During heavy rainfall these pipes could not discharge water quickly enough, causing rainwater to rise above the outlets and seep through cracks into the galleries below.

In January 2002, the Commonwealth Institute's statutory activities were formally brought to an end. Freed from its public obligations, the organization's site passed ownership to an independent charitable trust. However, the cost of maintaining the building was now unsustainable. The countries of the Commonwealth resolved to sell the building, with the proceeds being used to advance education across the Commonwealth. In 2004, the building closed its doors to the public and was sold a few years later.

In 2012, photographer Koto Bolofo was invited to document the building's conversion into the new Design Museum [30–32]. Bolofo used a traditional analogue camera and film to record the building before work started. He went on to trace the laborious process needed to prop the building while floors were removed. What Bolofo captured was a picturesque mid-century ruin, that stood as a reflection of the fragile nature of modernity. However, the dilapidated state of the former Institute

32

32 Stained glass from the Commonwealth Institute was
restored and relocated to the Design Museum shop.

should not be seen as a metaphor for the supposedly declining significance of the Commonwealth itself, which has proved to be a surprisingly resilient association.

The Design Museum's conversion of the former Commonwealth Institute has restored to public use one of the most important post-war buildings in London. Visitors can enjoy the roof's sculptural qualities once again, and the building's complicated history also allows the museum to engage with alternative understandings about what design might mean. The Commonwealth Institute's complex legacy reminds us that design not only shapes the world, but it also shapes our common understanding of the world and our place in it.

the making
of a new museum

1

1   The original dais and central void, photographed at the outset of the architectural competition to transform the building, 2010

Living as I do in West London, the former Commonwealth Institute building—the iconic 'tent in the park'—has long been a marker in my mental map of the city. Radical when it was originally designed—a triple-height exhibition hall, over-flown by an aggrandized hyperbolic-paraboloid roof—the daringness of the form is still apparent to me every time I drive, cycle or walk past. I am conscious of how fortunate it is to have had my first major public project located so close to home. There is no substitute for the intensity of engagement that sustained intimacy with a place brings.

Shortly after the suggestion was first made that this landmark of post-war British Modernism could become the new permanent home of the Design Museum, I walked through the deserted site with the director, Deyan Sudjic. In a narrative repeated countless times since the queen opened the building on 6 November 1962, we passed through the low entry area, emerging onto the dais and into the central void, below the dramatic thrust and span of the roof. The transition from spatial compression to spatial expansion was exhilarating: something experienced visually, viscerally and mentally. When we had climbed the final flight of stairs to the top floor, the highest extended curve still swept up another 16 metres [1–3]. Even empty, it was possible to imagine the space reworked and repopulated, a place through which one would circulate as through an opencast mine, with the journey animated by points of interest at every turn—not just individual exhibits and glimpses into gallery spaces, but views of the museum's library and working areas.

We have become accustomed to the idea of architects repurposing decommissioned industrial buildings for cultural uses. It might seem that the prospect of turning one defunct museum into another, different museum would be a less complex undertaking—less demanding, for example, than transforming a power station into an art gallery. From that very first visit, however, it was clear to me that the challenges here, while undoubtedly exciting, would also be profound, particularly in relation to the engineered character of the structure and to the task of uniting the given volume with the required programme. How would it be possible to combine so grand an architectural gesture with the need to get the spatial thinking

2

3

2   The dilapidated fabric of the entrance area, 2010. The world map was relocated from the entrance to the Institute, and is now positioned in the foyer of the Bakala auditorium.

3   At its highest points the dynamic geometry of the roof rises 16 metres above the building's upper floor.

right—to make beautiful, contemporary environments for temporary exhibitions, for the museum's permanent collection, for education and for all the many functions of an institution of this stature?

Ever since, as a teenager, I organized the removal of the first of a series of walls in my parents' house in Yorkshire to improve the proportions of my bedroom, I have been interested in making spaces in which people feel comfortable and where the eye can move freely, based on the qualities of light and materials. Since these simple, pared-back spaces are also sympathetic environments for art, it is perhaps unsurprising that a number of my first professional commissions were for galleries. The quality that marked out these early projects was the near invisibility of the architecture. Looking back over the photographs, it is the Flanagan horse or the Calder mobile that you register. Only later might you notice the detail of the junction between the wall and the floor, or the grain of the timber boarding. That was the point. The focus was all on the art [4–6].

Invisible architecture – a quiet visual field – was never going to be an option in the former Commonwealth Institute building, within so exuberant an existing frame: on the contrary, my instinct was that the inherited spirit of architectural boldness would be something to strengthen and enhance, rather than mute. In any case, a museum of design is very different from an art gallery. But there was opportunity, I felt, to simplify some aspects of the spaces; to think deeply about the quality of the light, the surfaces, the details of the proportions and the acoustics, as well as significantly redrawing the choreography, so that the all the patterns of circulation—for visitors and those for whom the building would be a regular workplace—would feel natural and instinctive.

An attitude to the display of objects has to be at the heart of a museum of design. The physical environment of such a place does not simply provide a context for this attitude, it should both define and be defined by it. The interior architecture must offer the means to circulate, to eat, to buy, to work, to learn and to store but, above all else, it must embody a view of how to place and experience objects in space—objects of diverse scales and typologies, requiring a range of climatic and lighting

4

5

6

4   One of the spatial interventions designed for *The Raw and the Cooked* exhibition in the Museum of Modern Art, Oxford, 1994

5   The quiet visual field at the Waddington Gallery, London, 1984

6   PPOW Gallery, New York, 1986. The space was created from an industrial interior in the Lower East Side.

7

7   *Plain Space* at the Fondazione Bisazza, near Vicenza, northern Italy, 2012. This site-specific 1:1 structure was a recurring element of the touring exhibition.

conditions. At the Kensington site, there is inbuilt resonance in the fact that the Commonwealth Institute not only occupied a radical form, it also embodied, in its time, innovative conceptual thinking in terms of educational and exhibition techniques. Ways of showing have changed dramatically since then. The Commonwealth Institute was framed for a very particular form of display that was intended to be non-hierarchical and heavily didactic. Neither of these is a defining curatorial priority of the Design Museum—which also has a rolling programme of exhibitions, where the Commonwealth Institute's installation was set up on a permanent basis.

I don't do many competitions, but when I finally made the decision to enter this one, in an important sense my relationship with the building began again. Every reflection was suddenly charged with possibility; every musing came with an awareness of consequences. Competitions require mental adjustment. Emotionally, it is difficult to embark on a process knowing that the narrative may be only partial, but on the other hand these can be the very circumstances that help keep the thinking fresh. Where my instinct with a new project is generally to refine and to push as far as possible into the actual detail, in a competition it is all about the ideas and communication of the ideas. You want to give people a real sense of what it will be like to be in a place, at a stage when the spaces exist only in your head. To achieve this, we used models, photographs and sketches, but we also tried to convey some of the atmosphere of the place with words.

It was relevant to the direction of my thinking that, during the early phases of the design work, I took adaptations of the *Plain Space* exhibition of my work—originally shown at the Design Museum in Shad Thames, on the other side of London—first to the Pinakothek der Moderne in Munich and then to Bisazza in Vicenza [7–9]. These experiences brought home to me with renewed force, the significance of the spaces around things in exhibiting environments. The content of each show varied only slightly, but the experience for the visitor was different every time—even for me—because the spatial relationships were different. Each successive installation brought fresh insights and perspectives,

8

9

8 1:1 interior, Pinakothek der Moderne, Munich, 2012
9 1:1 interior, created for the Design Museum at its former
   location in Shad Thames, where the *Plain Space*
   exhibition originally opened in 2010

and allowed new connections to be made. It deepened my understanding that the work of an architect overlaps significantly with the roles of curator and editor. So much relies on the refinement of the choices you make: of what you put in, of what you leave out and of precisely where you choose to place things. At the Design Museum, I wanted to offer simple backdrops – clear visual arenas – but places with scope for atmosphere and for this richness of spatial relationship.

Intense though the architectural process immediately became, I wanted to find a way to work with a light hand. It was important to me that the outcome would not be experienced as a fracture with the past. At the end of the project, I wanted it to feel as though the building had somehow retuned itself, allowing future generations a new and intense engagement with something that had essentially always been there. Above all, the thought I found myself coming back to again and again was that exhilarating sense of vertical expansion I had on first stepping into the heart of the floor plan.

Significant, of course, to the direction of the design thinking was the building's conservation status. The Commonwealth Institute was classified Grade II* in 1988, a designation reserved for buildings judged to be 'particularly important … of more than special interest'. In this case, the listing was given specifically in recognition of the structure's roof, its place as a post-war building, its importance in the history of museum and exhibition design and its historical significance in marking the transition from empire to commonwealth. English Heritage's stated conservation priorities included the roof structure and buttresses, the tiered internal spaces and sense of spatial progression experienced by the visitor, the prominence of the central platform, the top-lit quality and enclosed nature of the interior space and the dramatic sweep of the concrete-shell roof.

At the same time, it was impressed upon us at the earliest stages of the design process that the impact of the listing should not be to fix the building in amber. In *Conservation Principles: Policies and Guidance*, published in 2008, English Heritage acknowledges value in successive acts of repossession:

10

10   The museum is orientated at a 45-degree angle to
      Kensington High Street.

change to a significant place is inevitable...keeping a significant place in use is likely to require continual adaptation and change...The work of successive generations often contributes to [their] significance. Owners and managers of significant places should not be discouraged from adding further layers of potential future interest and value.

Similarly, the Government Planning Policy Guidance notes observe that:

Many listed buildings can sustain some degree of sensitive alteration or extension to accommodate continuing or new uses. Indeed cumulative changes reflecting the history of use and ownership are themselves an aspect of the special interest of some buildings, and the merit of some new alterations or additions, especially where they are generated within a secure and committed long-term ownership, should not be discounted.

This process of evolution and adjustment—of 'adding further layers'—began with decisions about the exterior of the structure and the character of its engagement with the contrasting elements of its setting. To the north and east, the great expanse of Holland Park wraps the museum plot, while OMA's new apartment buildings located in landscape by the Dutch designers West 8—schemes that were still only on paper when we began our own conceptual design work—provide its context to the west and south. Also pertinent was the decision taken by the architects of the original scheme to orientate the structure at a 45-degree angle to the street, setting up unusual rhythms and interactions whose impact became clearer as we thought about how to strengthen the Design Museum's presence on Kensington High Street and create the best possible journeys from all points into the heart of the building [10].

A defining ambition of the broader vision for the site was the idea of completely recalibrating the relationship between architecture, park and public, to make something far more fluid than had previously been the case. Within the constraints associated with the building's

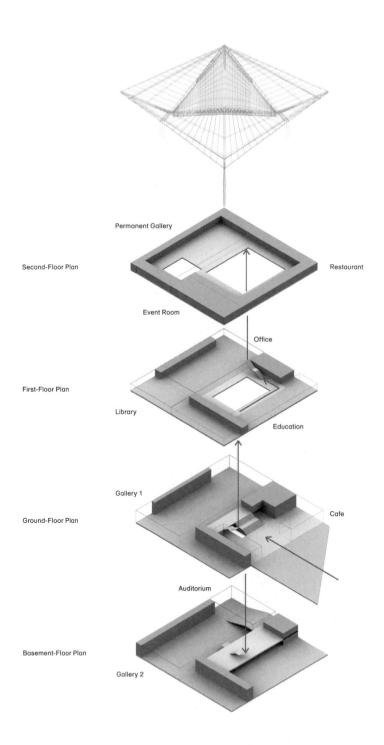

Permanent Gallery

Second-Floor Plan

Restaurant

Event Room

Office

First-Floor Plan

Library

Education

Gallery 1

Ground-Floor Plan

Cafe

Auditorium

Basement-Floor Plan

Gallery 2

11   Exploded axonometric showing the different floors of
the museum above and below ground

listing, our design reworked the ground floor as permeable territory through which people can move from the green spaces of the park in a relaxed and instinctive manner, with new glazed openings to the foyer and the original stained-glass windows, previously installed on the south facade, relocated to the north, next to the new entrance from Holland Park.

In line with this wider design strategy for openness, a significant change to the appearance of the building is that its skin has become transparent on the north and east elevations, meaning that people in the park can look in on the life of the museum and vice versa. This is very much in the spirit of the architects' original concept of the building as a 'tent in the park': as I see it, we're just opening the flaps of the tent. New translucent panels introduced into the south and west facades continue this theme and serve the functional purpose of increasing levels of natural light in the education and office spaces, reducing the amount of artificial lighting required in these areas during the day—issues of sustainability are relevant to all projects, and here we started on a good footing in the sense that we have reused an existing building.

Studying the structure—as a physical space, and on paper—it was obvious that the atrium should be left open and that the build-out should be restrained in character. In the existing building, the central concrete section of the roof rose up through the volume on two structural supports, and arched over the central space before curving back down towards the middle floor. The floor slab opened up around the structure, allowing it to pass through to the floor below. To preserve this defining feature, we have created two openings in the new top-floor slab. The larger opening relates to the central void, and the smaller one visually connects the Sackler Library on the first floor to the permanent exhibition space. The creation of the second opening allows further views up to the roof from the first-floor level, as well as creating a sightline into the workings of the museum for people visiting the permanent exhibitions on the second floor. The central void visually and physically connects all the public levels of the building, and recreates the sense of a single volume and tiered levels that characterized the original interior configuration [11–15].

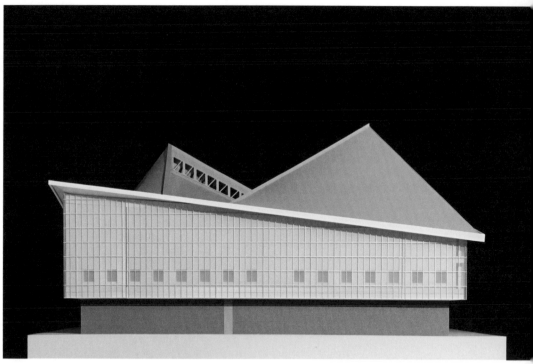

12

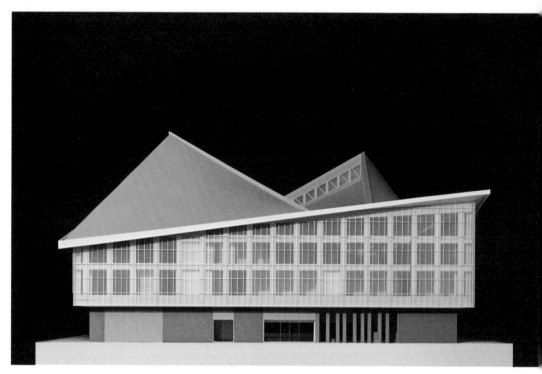

13

14

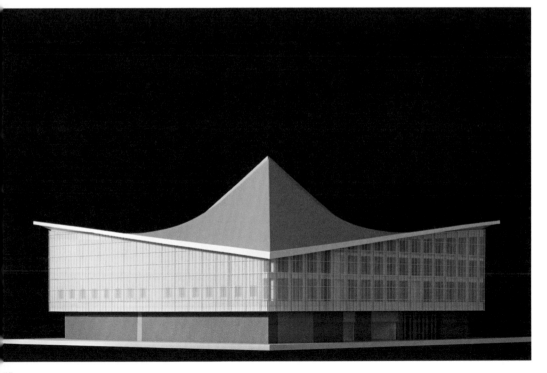

15

16

12–15   1:43 physical model of the new Design Museum
16   The entire structure was propped on piles during
excavation of the basement levels, 2013.

A key part of the design rationale was that the floor slabs be clearly expressed as strong, horizontal elements. The slab edges are therefore finished in white, as in the original building, contrasting with the timber walls and defining the volumes of the first and second floors. To reinforce this idea, all the volumes, including the lift cores on the top floor, are located around the perimeter of the building. When you enter the new museum, you instinctively look up through the central void, orientate yourself and feel the anti-gravitational pull of the roof structure, just as the architects of the original building intended.

Excavation for the large double-height basement and upper-basement mezzanine level provided the most dramatic phase of the construction period, as it required the entire building—including the original roof structure—to be propped on stilts. A series of piles, temporary beams and trusses was built around and through the existing structure to bear the internal roof-support columns and the roof-edge-support mullions [16]. The existing external walls and internal structure were then demolished, and the new structure built up around the temporary works until it could carry the roof. Only then were the temporary supports removed and the new structure completed, allowing the fit-out work to commence [17].

For an architect, it is a great privilege to watch a building's gradual transformation over a period of years, as the spaces and surfaces one has in one's head begin to become physical reality. When we started taking bits of the building away, we inevitably found that the construction was not exactly as we had expected, which slowed things down. There were periods when progress appeared painfully slow, and brief intervals when it ceased altogether while unforeseen issues were resolved. At times, the structure appeared raw and melancholy, at others charged with a sort of poetry—as when the site of the excavation resembled some vast piece of marine archaeology.

For six intense years, helping to create a new home for the Design Museum was a huge part of my life and that of my office. Over that period, the many-layered dialogue ebbed and flowed, through easier and more taxing periods. There is a great deal of talking in architecture and no shortcut for time spent with others round

17

17 Progress on site, fourteen months after the ceremony
marking the breaking of ground, 2013

a table as opposed to solitarily at one's desk: indeed, in my experience, the quality of a finished project generally corresponds directly to the quality of the conversations. In this case, the numbers involved were particularly large, encompassing the many individuals that make up the staff of a substantial contemporary museum; the architectural team at OMA; the landscape architects; exhibition designers; the local planners; English Heritage; the extensive consultant team; the developers; and, later on, the numerous contractors involved on site. My exchanges with Roger Cunliffe, a member of the original architectural team, proved a particular pleasure and privilege. It has also been fascinating watching how the different photographers who have spent time on the site at various stages have each come away with a personal perspective—each eye, each lens capturing its own unique way of looking.

Without question, this undertaking will form a defining mark in the body of my work—as well as in the collective experience of the team, some of whom grew up around the capital and remember visiting the former Commonwealth Institute as schoolchildren. Whenever people ask me which commission I view as my most important—which they so frequently do—my reflex response is to name whatever is currently on my desk: when one is immersed in a project, past and future tend to recede. The Design Museum is different, however, not least because I suspect the state of immersive engagement will never truly end. Like the houses I have made for my own family, geographical proximity means that I will be perpetually revisiting the design decisions and reviewing the details. In this sense, as in others, I can honestly say that the Design Museum will remain the project of a lifetime.

18

18   Excavation of the basement levels, beneath the
propped interior structure, 2013
19   Completed concrete floor slab and steel stair
structure, 2015

20

20　The new top floor takes shape under the original roof
　　braces, 2015.
21　New stainless-steel-clad rainwater routes are located
　　on the upper faces of the roof buttresses, 2015.
22　Work advances on the lift core, as the formwork for the
　　new concrete structure is prepared, 2015.

21

22

23

24

25

25–26 The atrium space is lined out, while work continues on
the mezzanine and stairs, 2016
27 Stained glass from the original building, designed by
Keith New and restored by John Reyntiens, installed in
its new permanent location near the atrium shop, 2016.

26

27

Hélène Binet
photographs the museum

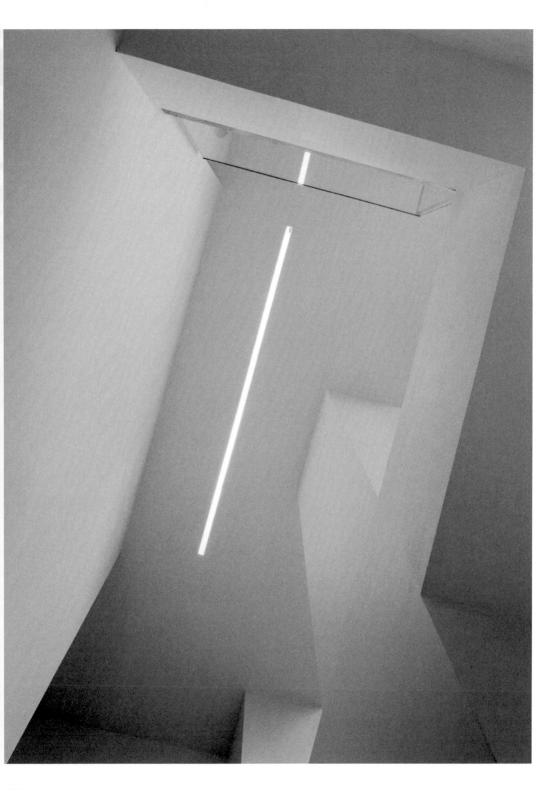

further information
and index

Boilerhouse Project Exhibitions

1982 Art and Industry: A Century of Design
         in the Products We Use
      Sony Design
      Royal Flush: A Celebration of 100 Years
         of the Water-Closet
      Design: Dieter Rams
      The Car Programme: 52 Months to Job One,
         or how they designed the Ford Sierra
      Memphis: Milano in London

1983 Design: The Problem Comes First
      Kenneth Grange at the Boilerhouse:
         An Exhibition of British Product Design
      Images for Sale
      Taste: An Exhibition about Values in Design
      Philip Garner's 'Better Living' Exhibition

1984 Hand Tools: The Culture of Manual Work
      Design at Kingston
      Robots
      Post Modern Colour

1985 The Good Design Guide: 100 Best Ever Products
      Issey Miyake: Bodyworks
      National Characteristics in Design
      The Bag
      The Car
      Natural Design: The Search for Comfort
         and Efficiency

1986 Coke! Coca-Cola, 1886–1986:
         Designing a Mega-Brand
      New Design for Old
      14:24: British Youth Culture

Shad Thames Exhibitions

1989 Commerce and Culture: From Pre-industrial Art
         to Post-industrial Value
      French Design
      The Best of British Graphics
      10 Years of Eau
      FIAT Posters
      Corporate Identity

1990 Sport 90: Design and Sport
      Devětsil: Czech Avant-Garde Art, Architecture
         and Design of the 1920s and 30s
      Graphic Design in America:
         A Visual Language History
      Design in the Public Service:
         The Dutch PTT 1920–1990
      Contemporary Spanish Graphic Design
      Mario Sironi: Advertising Graphics
      Abram Games: 60 Years of Design
      Hans Schleger

1991 Alfa Romeo: Sport through Design
      Raymond Loewy: Pioneer of American
         Industrial Design
      Designing Yourself? Creativity in Everyday Life
      Metropolis: Tokyo Design Visions
      Chinese Graphic Design
      FHK Henrion 1914–1990
      New Japanese Graphics
      The Material World of Tintin
      Citroën DS
      Organic Design
      Eye Spy: Sub-Miniature Cameras

1992 Eileen Gray
      Base over Apex: The Decline of
         the British Motorcycle
      Scandinavian Festival: New Directions
         in Scandinavian Design

1993 Malcolm Garrett: Ulterior Motifs
      The 2nd Moulinex Generation Student Competition
      Type and Image
      Scandinavian Design in Britain
      More Mileage: Car Design for Elderly
         and Disabled People
      Cinquecento! 60 Years of City-Car Design
      OMK: The Designs of Rodney Kinsman
      Frank Gehry: New Bentwood Furniture Designs
      Is Starck a Designer?

1994 CFA Voysey: Heart and Home
      Detached Dreams: Ideal Homes
      The MuZ Motorbike: Developing a New Product
      RSA Student Design Awards
      Conran Foundation Collection: Ross Lovegrove
      Tokyo Design Network Showcase
      Grafica Utile: Italian Posters of Social Information,
         Protest and Celebration 1975–1993
      50 Years of Poster Design: G & B Arts

Designed in One, Made in the Other:
   New Products of Collaboration between
   Britain and Japan
Arne Jacobsen
It's Plastic!

1995   It's 100% Man-Made
Conran Foundation Collection:
   Jasper Morrison Work/Shop
Frank Lloyd Wright in Chicago: The Early Years
Paul Smith: True Brit
Alessi: Family Follows Fiction Showcase
60/90: The Inheritance of the Sixties
Thinkteck! Tokyo Design Network/Design
   Museum Research Project
Paper Money
Designing Messages: European Stamp Design
Conran Foundation Collection: Alice Rawsthorn

1996   100 Masterpieces: The Furniture that
   made the Twentieth Century
Fabergé
Charlotte Perriand: Modernist Pioneer
Doing a Dyson
Conran Foundation Collection: Janice Kirkpatrick

1997   The Power of Erotic Design
The Coca-Cola Bottle
Conran Foundation Collection: Dan Pearson
Bike: Cycles, a tour of bicycle design 1825–2000

1998   Ferdinand Porsche: Design Dynasty
Innovation by Design: 100 Years of Bosch in the UK
The Real David Mellor
The Work of Charles and Ray Eames:
   A Legacy of Invention
Conran Foundation Collection: David Constantine

1999   Modern Britain 1929–1939
Mini: 40 Years of a Design Icon
Verner Panton: Light and Colour
The Appeal of Reason
On the Road: The Art of Engineering in the Car Age
Rado
Design Now: Austria
Design: Process, Progress, Practice

2000   Living in the City
Movement: Peter Opsvik
Bauhaus Dessau
Under a Fiver
Kind Of Blue
Dr. Martens
Zoeftig
Marc Newson's Ford 021C
Buckminster Fuller: Your Private Sky
Six Moments
New Design and Technology
Waves
Equilibrium
Pierre Cardin: Sculptures Utilitaires

Conran Foundation Collection: Tyler Brûlé
Isambard Kingdom Brunel: Recent Works
Design Against Crime

2001   What About Design?
Minor Works: Designing for Children
Luis Barragán
Communicating Design
Isamu Noguchi
Memphis Remembered
A World Without Words, Jasper Morrison
Aston Martin
Dirty Washing
Conran Foundation Collection: Marc Newson
Web Wizards: Designers Who Define the Web

2002   Ronan and Erwan Bouroullec
Leopold and Rudolf Blaschka: The Glass Aquarium
Arne Jacobsen: Cocktails With Arne
Gio Ponti: A World
Paul Smith's Robots
Rainer & Martino's World Cup
Leopold and Rudolph Blaschka:
   The Glass Menagerie
Design Now: Graphics
Ford Thunderbirds
When Philip Met Isabella: Philip Treacy's
   Hats for Isabella Blow
The Digital Aquarium
A Century of Chairs
Jerszy Seymour
The Adventures of Aluminium: From Jewellery to Jets
Unseen Vogue
Living in a Tank: Sleeping
Christophe Seyferth
Conran Foundation Collection: Droog

2003   The MARS Group
Klein Dytham
Manolo Blahnik
A Century of Chairs
Superstudio: Life Without Objects
The Peter Saville Show
Living in a Tank: Working
Wild Silk, Tord Boontje
Hella Jongerius
Sam Buxton
When Flaminio Drove to France:
   Flaminio Bertoni's Designs for Citröen
Somewhere Totally Else: The European Design Show
Abram Games
History of Modern Design: In the Home
The One-Legged Milk Stool
Alison and Peter Smithson: House of
   Tomorrow to a House for Today

2004   Conran Foundation Collection: Thomas Heatherwick
Styrenissimo, Paul Cocksedge
Archigram
Plant Power, Ronan and Erwan Bouroullec
A Century of Chairs

Designer of the Year

2003 Jonathan Ive
2004 Daniel Brown
2005 Hilary Cottam
2006 Gorillaz

Designs of the Year

2008 One Laptop Per Child
Yves Béhar of fuseproject, USA
2009 Barack Obama poster
Shepard Fairey, USA
2010 Folding Plug
Min-Kyu Choi, UK
2011 Plumen 001
Hulger and Samuel Wilkinson, UK
2012 London 2012 Olympic Torch
Edward Barber and Jay Osgerby for the London
Organising Committee of the Olympic and Paralympic
Games, UK
2013 GOV.UK website
Government Digital Service, UK
2014 Heydar Aliyev Cultural Centre
Zaha Hadid Architects, UK, for the Republic
of Azerbaijan
2015 Human Organs-on-Chips
Donald Ingber and Dan Dongeun Huh at Harvard
University's Wyss Institute, USA

Designers in Residence

2007 Tomás Alonso
Sarah van Gameren
Finn Magee
Chris O'Shea
Richard Sweeney

2008 *Collecting/Collections*
Sarah Angold
Tom Drysdale
Matthew Falla
Lea Jagendorf
Jethro Macey
Ben Storan
Adrian Westaway
Freddie Yauner

2009/2010 *Networks*
Dave Bowker
Farm Collective: Guy Brown, Alexena Cayless,
Giles Miller and Sebastian Hejna
Asif Khan
Marc Owens
Bethan Laura Wood

2011 *In Pursuit of Imperfection*
Jade Folawiyo
Simon Hasan
Hye-Yeon Park
Will Shannon

2012 *Thrift*
Lawrence Lek
Freyja Sewell
Yuri Suzuki
Harry Trimble
Oscar Medley Whitfield

2013 *Identity*
Adam Nathaniel Furman
Eunhee Jo
Chloe Meineck
Thomas Thwaites

2014 *Disruption*
James Christian
Ilona Gaynor
Torsten Sherwood
Patrick Stevenson-Keating

2015 *Migration*
Chris Green
Stephanie Hornig
Hefin Jones
Alexa Pollmann

2016 *Open*
Alix Bizet
Clementine Blakemore
Andrea de Chirico
Rain Wu

Index

O

Olivetti 25
Olympus cameras 41
OMA 97, 105
One Laptop Per Child project *44*
Orrery Bar, London 17, *18*
Oxford
    Museum of Modern Art *90*

P

Panton, Verner *39*, 41
Paris 11
    Pompidou Centre 21
The Past, Present and Future of Sony (1982) *26*
Pawson, John 9, 12, *27*, 49, 87–105
Perriand, Charlotte 41
Perry, Herry *56*
Philips Pavilion, Brussels World's Fair (1958) 65
Pinakothek der Moderne, Munich 93, *94*
Plain Space, Vicenza (2012) *92*, 93
Pompidou Centre, Paris 21
Pope-Hennessy, Sir John 12
Porsche, Ferdinand *39*, 41
Potter's Field, London 49
The Power of Erotic Design (1997) *38*
PPOW Gallery, New York *91*

Q

Quant, Mary *19*

R

Rams, Dieter 45
The Raw and the Cooked exhibition, Oxford (1994) *90*
Rawsthorn, Alice 41–5
Readymoney, Cowasji Jehangir 71
Rees, Helen 37, 41
Reilly, Paul 7–8, 9, 21
Reyntiens, John *113*
Robert Matthew Johnson-Marshall & Partners (RMJM)
    61–73, *64*
Roussel, Raphael *55*
Royal Albert Hall, London 53
Royal College of Art, London 21, 61
Royal Festival Hall, London 61, 69
Royal Horticultural Society 55

S

Sackler Library 99
Sapper, Richard 33
Sassoon, Vidal *19*
Saville, Peter 41
Schleger, Hans 37

Shad Thames

Shad Thames 8–9, 12, *28*, 29–49, *30–1*
Singapore 77
Smith, Paul *43*, 45
Sony 25
    Walkman 33
Sottsass, Ettore 25, *42*, 45
Soup Kitchen, London 17
South Bank, London 61
Spooner, Herbert 57
Spry, Constance 45
Starck, Philippe 41
Strong, Sir Roy 8, 23
Sturgis, Tim 61
Sudjic, Deyan 9, 11–13, 45, 87
Sutherland, James 61, 65, 69
Sydney Opera House 65

T

Tasmania 73
Tate Gallery, London 21
Tate Modern, London 49
Teague, Walter Dorwin 25
Teese, Dita von *43*
Thames, River 29
Thatcher, Margaret *32*, 33
Thompson, Paul 41
Tower Bridge, London 29

U

Uganda 73
Underground Group *56*
University of London 57
Unseen Vogue (2002) *40*
Urquiola, Patricia 45
Utzon, Jørn 65

V

Verner Panton: Light and Colour (1999) *39*, 41
Vicenza
    Fondazione Bisazza *92*, 93
Victoria, Queen 53
Victoria and Albert Museum, London 11, 23, 49
    Boilerhouse Project 8, 11–12, *20*, 23–9
Vienna 11
Vogue 40
Vorderman, Carole 41

W

Waddington Gallery, London *91*
Webb, Aston 23
West Africa 73
West 8 97
Willen Lake, Milton Keynes 21–3

Contributor Biographies

Hélène Binet (1959) is a world-renowned architectural photographer whose work explores both contemporary and historical landmarks. Binet began her career photographing performances for the Geneva Opera House, before turning her focus to the work of contemporary architects such as Zaha Hadid and Daniel Libeskind. She has published books on the iconic works of Alvar Aalto, Sigurd Lewerentz and Le Corbuiser. Binet is currently represented by the ammann// gallery in Germany, displaying her work in solo exhibitions and at international art fairs. Since 2014 Binet's photographs have belonged to the permanent collection of the Museum of Modern Art in New York and the Carnegie Museum of Art in Pittsburgh, Pennsylvania.

Terence Conran (1931) is a designer, entrepreneur and the founder of the Design Musem who has worked widely throughout Europe, Japan and America. His brand of affordable, design-conscious homewear is credited with the introduction of contemporary design to the British retail mainstream. Conran studied at the Central School of Art and Design and began his career in 1951 as an architectural assistant working on displays for the Festival of Britain. In 1964, he opened the first of many Habitat stores, selling a range of household goods and furniture. In 1980, Conran established the architectural and planning consultancy firm Conran Roche, followed by a number of other business in the worlds of publishing, retail, furniture and manufacturing. His restaurants have also had an important impact on contemporary dining culture. Conran was knighted in 1983.

John Pawson (1949) has spent over thirty years making rigorously simple architecture that is rooted in a consistent set of preoccupations with mass, volume, surface, proportion, junction, geometry, repetition, light and ritual. His body of work spans a broad range of scales and typologies, including houses, sacred commissions, galleries, museums, hotels, ballet sets, yacht interiors and a lake crossing. As Alvar Aalto's bronze door handle has been characterized as the 'handshake of a building', so a sense of engaging with the essence of a philosophy of space through everything the eye sees or the hand touches is a defining aspect of Pawson's designs. An exhibition of his work was held at the Design Museum in 2010.

Deyan Sudjic (1952) was appointed as the director the Design Museum in 2006. He began his career as founding editor of the architectural journal *Blueprint* in 1983; subsequently working as editor of *Domus* magazine from 2000 to 2004. His influence in the field of design and architecture has spanned teaching, journalism and publishing. He was also appointed director of the Venice Architecture Biennale in 2002. Sudjic has published many books on design and architecture including *The Edifice Complex* (2005), *The Language of Things* (2008), *Norman Foster: A Life in Architecture* (2010), *Shiro Kuramata* (2013) and *B is for Bauhaus* (2014). His most recent, *Ettore Sottsass and the Poetry of Things*, was published by Phaidon in 2015. Sudjic was honored as an OBE in 2000 in recognition of his contribution to the arts.

Tom Wilson (1979) is head of collection and research at the Design Museum in London. Prior to joining the museum, Wilson taught Critical and Contextual Studies at the London Metropolitan University. Following which in 2013, he held a post as curator in residence at the National Institute of Design in Ahmedabad as part of the British Council's Design Curation Program in India. In 2016, Wilson completed his AHRC-funded PhD on the design and display strategies of the Commonwealth Institute: the Design Museum's new home.

Acknowledgements

Design Museum design team:
John Pawson
Arup
ChapmanBDSP
Turner & Townsend
Gardiner & Theobald LLP
Tricon Limited

Signage:
Cartlidge Levene

Restaurant:
Universal Design Studio

Permanent installation:
Studio Myerscough

Developer:
Chelsfield Group Ltd in collaboration
with the Ilchester Estates

Developer's design team:
OMA
Allies and Morrison
West 8
Arup and AECOM

Developer's contractor:
MACE

Fit-out contractor:
Willmott Dixon Interiors

Exhibition installation:
Elmwood

Retail:
Vitra

Furniture:
Vitra

Bars:
Benchmark

Lighting:
Concord

Founding Funders:
Arts Council England
Atkin Foundation
Zdenek and Michaela Bakala
The Conran Foundation
Sir Terence Conran
Sir John Hegarty and Miss Philippa Crane
Heritage Lottery Fund
Helene and Johannes Huth
Dr Mortimer and Theresa Sackler Foundation
Swarovski Foundation

Campaign Donors:
29th May 1961 Charitable Trust, Eric Abraham, Aram
Designs Limited, Chumsri and Luqman Arnold, Wendy
Becker, Belvedere Trust, The Bernard Sunley Charitable
Foundation, Nicholas and Katusha Bull, Jennifer Butler,
Calvin Klein Inc, Jehan Pei-Chung Chu, Concord, Neville
and Carole Conrad, Sebastian Conran, David Constantine
MBE, Mike Davis, Miel de Botton, Department of Culture
Media and Sport, Hugh Devlin, Nicoletta Fiorucci, Sir
Christopher Frayling, Loic le Gaillard, Piero Gandini,
Garfield Weston Foundation, Professor Naomi Gornick
FCSD, Richard and Judith Greer, The Grocers' Charity,
The Hans and Marit Rausing Charitable Trust, Ian and
Morny Hay Davison, Anya Hindmarch MBE, Hintze Family
Charitable Foundation, Isabelle and Mark Hotimsky,
J. Paul Getty Jnr Charitable Trust, John Young Charitable
Settlement, Alistair D. K. Johnston CMG, Asif Kahn, Kirby
Laing Foundation, Marie Joseé and Henry R Kravis, Michael
Likierman, Philip and Davina Mallinckrodt, Ambra Medda,
Lee F. Mindel FAIA, Jon Moynihan, Saba Nazar, Nicholas
Norton, John Ormerod, Phillips, Paul Priestman, Debra
Reuben, Charles Rifkind, Lady Ritblat, Royal Commission
for the Exhibition of 1851, Rolf Sachs, The Sackler Trust,
Schroder Foundation, Segal Family Foundation, Shelton
Mindel and Associates, Sir Siegmund Warburg's Voluntary
Settlement, Sir Paul Smith, Stavros Niarchos Foundation,
Maria and Malek Sukkar, Tallow Chandlers Company,
Suzanna Taverne, Julian and Louisa Treger, Melissa Ulfane,
United Children of the World Charitable Trust, Vitra, Julian
Vogel, Waste Recycling Environment Ltd., Yvonne and Pierre
Winkler, Wolfson Foundation.

*The Design Museum thanks its board of trustees for their
continued support.*

Hélène Binet's photographs of the Design Museum were
taken with the assistance of Ben Thomas and Alessandra
Trainiti. Access was made possible with the kind support of
Michael Ayres, Yvette Chin, Xavier Paris and Julia Ravenscroft.

The author would like to thank Mark Cortes Favis and Michael
Radford for their unfailing support and good humour, and
Villalba Lawson for their attention to detail in putting this
book together. Many colleagues at the Design Museum have
contributed to this book, and thanks go to them all. Special
acknowledgements go to Catherine Moriarty, Helen Charman,
Anita Rupprecht and Donna Loveday for their constant
support, encouragement and guidance.

Picture Credits

Unless otherwise noted, all images are courtesy and copyright © the Design Museum.

John Andrews: 91 (l)
Arcaid Images: 36
Archigram Archives University of Westminster: 78
Architectural Press Archive/RIBA Collections: 72 (b), 76
© BLW: 47
Flo Bayley: 20 (b), 22
Hélène Binet: 82, 116–37
Bristol Museums, Galleries and Archives: British Empire and Commonwealth Collections: 55, 72 (t)
Central Office of Information: 60
Stafford Cliff: 26
© Tim Davey: 48
David Davies: 34
© Richard Davies: 43 (tr)
Mike Dempsey: 38 (t)
Design Studio Myerscough: 42 (tl)
Ian Dobbie: 27 (r), 90
© Terence Donovan/Trunk Archive: 18 (br)
Brian Duffy/Vogue © The Condé Nast Publications Ltd: 40 (tr)
© GTF: 40 (b)
Getty: 20 (t)
Max Gleeson: 110–13
Habitat Retail Limited: 19
© Koto Bolofo: 80
© Luke Hayes: 42 (b, tr), 43 (b, tl)
Poul Ib Henriksen: 39
Historic England Archive: 30 (tl)
Historic England Archive (John Laing Collection): 62, 64, 66, 67, 68
The Imperial Institute of the United Kingdom, The Colonies and India: 54 (t)
Gilbert McCarragher: 86, 88, 94 (b), 96, 100–101, 102, 104, 106–109
Neville Miles: 58 (t)
James Moriarty: 46
Michael Mundy: 91 (r)
One Laptop Per Child: 44 (t)
Andy Paradise/Paradise Photo: 40 (tl)
Pentagram: 35
RIBA Collections: 54 (b)
RMJM: 58 (b)
Jefferson Smith: 38 (bl, br)
Henk Snoek/RIBA Collections: 70
The British Architect: 52
© TfL from the London Transport Museum collection: 56
University of Brighton Design Archives: 18 (tl), 71, 74, 75 (t)
Valentine Postcard Collection: 75 (b)
Jens Weber: 94 (t)
© Ray Williams: 16
Wyss Institute at Harvard University: 44 (b)
Marco Zanta: 92

Every reasonable effort has been made to acknowledge the ownership of copyright for photographs included in this volume. Any errors that may have occurred are inadvertent, and will be corrected in subsequent editions provided notification is sent in writing to the publisher.

Phaidon Press Limited
Regent's Wharf
All Saints Street
London N1 9PA

Phaidon Press Inc.
65 Bleecker Street
New York, NY 10012

www.phaidon.com

In partnership with
the Design Museum
224-238 Kensington High Street
London W8 6AG

designmuseum.org

First Published in 2016
© 2016 Phaidon Press Limited
Texts © 2016 the Design Museum

ISBN 978 0 7148 7253 7

A CIP Catalog record for this book is available from
the British Library and the Library of Congress.

Phaidon Press Limited
Commissioning Editor: Virginia McLeod
Project Editor: Robyn Taylor
Production Controller: Alenka Oblak
Designers: Villalba Lawson

the Design Museum
Publishing Manager: Mark Cortes Favis
Publishing Coordinator: Ianthe Fry
Picture Researchers: Michael Radford and
Anabel Navarro Llorens
Editorial Assistant: Hiba Alobaydi and Cat Gough

Printed in the UK